The Visitations

Kathryn Simmonds
The Visitations

SEREN

Seren is the book imprint of
Poetry Wales Press Ltd.
57 Nolton Street, Bridgend, Wales, CF31 3AE
www.serenbooks.com
Facebook: facebook.com/SerenBooks
Twitter: @SerenBooks

The right of Kathryn Simmonds to be identified as
the author of this work has been asserted in accordance
with the Copyright, Designs and Patents Act, 1988.

ISBN: 978-1-78172-116-2
ISBN e-book: 978-1-78172-149-0
Kindle: 978-1-78172-150-6

A CIP record for this title is available from the British Library.

The publisher acknowledges the financial assistance of the Welsh Books Council.

Cover photograph: Jean Pagliuso
from 'Poultry Suite' Buff #6 2010.
Silver gelatin print on handmade Kaji paper

Printed in Bembo by Bell and Bain, Glasgow

Contents

I

II

III

How do you change the weather in the blood?
– Elaine Feinstein

I

Sunday Morning

Since I've stopped praying
I've got so much more done:
the fridge is cleaner, I read more fiction,
the telephone is less often off the hook.
Since I've done away with God
I've done the bathroom up
and tried a dozen different recipes.

Since I've stopped considering the nature
of the soul, the infinite, all that,
I've found the joy of gardening;
I garden without concern
for the intricate glory of the Hollyhock.
The news is always on, the multitudes
keep dying, and what's one less prayer
circling the stratosphere?

He'll find me, if he chooses,
he'll lift me like a woolly two-year-old,
secure me to the fold. Meanwhile
I'm eating chocolates in bed,
the words of the psalms dissolving like an old dream,
I'm right here with a magazine,
– *Shock New Pictures, All Your TV Favourites* –
the church bells making a distant din,
the duvet warm and comforting,
the tumble dryer just spinning, and spinning.

Oversleeping

And there are the clothes you dropped, the arms of a green shirt
raised in surrender, the slough of nylon
                              and a dress of apricot wool.

Sit up and see the sheets fine-wired with pubic hair and eyelashes,
skin cells scattered like flakes of prehistory.

Your clothes have been going out of fashion,
quickly like the turning of a pear, slowly like a bone bleaching.
                              No matter,

reclaim the leather boots you loved so much,
zip them right up to the knee and walk;

you are Jairus' daughter, passing through
the convalescent house, its shelves of misremembered books,
                              its shivers of dust.

What else is there to do but open windows, let the outside
tumble in
like washing from a glorious machine?

The day is half over, but still blue. Step out and balance
on the ledge. Below a brown bird darts
                              over the garages
and is gone,
another yanks a worm from its clay bed and flies with it –
                              fly worm, fly!

The pillow-creases in your cheek smooth to make you young again.
Your leg hair stands to gold attention. Courage now, step out,

feel the plummet, then the catch and   you're up,
swimming in cold, eyes streaming.

There is the park where you broke your wrist, there is the church
where you first met God and the playground of children

whose children are running through cities now, as the river
runs, a silver speck, coursing underneath

the disappearing viaduct, running through the valley, past
fields where horses gather, trapped in their nature.

The houses reposition themselves
and there are your arms, the arms that used to be useless,
                                        parting pale belts of cloud.

April

Spring again
      But from where no telling
            Sweet as the spring
                  That went before

                  Same old story
           But still compelling
      Blossom reminding
What blossom is for

Question the trees
      But they're not telling
            How they obey
                An impossible law

                Question the mind
           But it's not telling
      How it gives back
What was gone for sure

Something stirs
      In a blacked-out dwelling
            Forces the lock
                Of a double-locked door

                  That face again!
           But from where no telling
      Sweet as the face
That was lost before

The New Mothers

They have mastered the buggy –
they understand the awkward catch,
what force of pressure makes it give.
They wheel with confidence, more
confidence, they wheel through afternoons
of amnesiac light, through mornings
loud with rain and evenings when
the sky is soothed to pink, thinking of
the secrets recently unshelled, the ones
their mothers kept so long, the bloody
songs of sealed rooms which day by day
grow faint and fainter still.
They pass by women being wheeled,
women sinking in their chairs who once
(can it be true?) sat small and snug
in carriage prams. Swelling women
pass by too, manoeuvring their mounds
they seem as far removed as first-year girls
to sixth-formers. And of course
they pass their kind, in cafes, parks –
half smiles, shy, as if they saw the nipples weep
inside each other's clothes. Another cup of tea;
they pause and redirect their gaze away,
beyond the complicated child they've made,
beyond the blurred pedestrians to girls
in skinny jeans, remembering how (again
impossibly) they *were* those girls,
the Matryoshka trick that had them
for a minute spotlit, arms raised
to glorify the tiny hours, sweat glittering
their foreheads – white light, noise –
and years away, unreachable through dancefloor mist,
babies with wet mouths feeding in the dark.

The Visitations

Sometimes God comes as a tiger,
And sometimes as a rose –
He opens for you secretly,
Perfuming your nose.

Sometimes he is a telephone,
Sometimes he is a key,
Sometimes he comes with hoola hoops,
Sometimes a dictionary.

Sometimes he comes as creosote
And leaves a nasty stain,
Sometimes he comes as anyone
Whose motives you can't name.

Sometimes he comes as sunlight –
Watch him tick across the wall.
And sometimes as a boxing glove.
And sometimes not at all.

On the Island of San Michele

We never thought to find the dead stacked up
in marble high-rises,

nor these photographs –
        a handsome man in his forties
                laughing into another year.

Six weeks –
                too soon to count you among the living;
one in five is lost, they say,
                        some say one in four.

September and the sky is freshly painted. Cyprus
scents the air.

Stravinsky and Diaghilev are here, graves strewn
        with offerings, not only flowers, but bread rings,
fancy candies melting in the heat.

        Ezra Pound eludes us.

A fellow tourist lifts his shades, points out Joseph Brodsky
at whose grave is fixed a letterbox.

        Too soon, and yet among the dead we play
        the naming game:

Benedicte?   Simone?

The hundred-year-old little girls
        stare poker-faced beneath their bows.

                        A lizard drips from a headstone.
                        My arms begin to burn.

Alicia?

Giving up the search for Pound, I lay my hand
on your plot instead: you buried alive
                              in your swirl of limbo.

        Nobone.   Wetstar.

I am waiting to row out on the nausea that must be coming –
                              like seasickness they say.

        From the quayside, Venice is a dot.

We buy unfamiliar chocolate from a snack machine
and I think of Petals
                    on a wet, black bough,

forming
        and falling
and forming.   And I ask you to live.

The Reluctant Natives

Fate landed us here by mistake, set us to walk
Welsh hillsides with a plodding heart
or paddle Essex estuaries under duress, our talk

always of somewhere else, (tacked to kitchen walls
a Swedish lake, a mountain range in Switzerland).
See us crouch in living rooms as daylight palls,

an old draft trespassing beneath the door, the trick
of day too quickly turning night, the radio's
relentless classic serial, that Sunday evening tick

of now becoming then. Hear us planning new
retreats, rephrasing sentences it takes
a lifetime to pronounce – *How nice to meet you*

in Hungarian, or *I'm from Hull* in faulty Greek –
curtains drawn against the rain, against
the pale countrymen to whom we rarely speak.

What I Did in My Summer Holidays

Never ask for an ice-cream confidently or menacingly or using
any other adverb. And if you're in pain, show me where it hurts
and how. Love is an abstract noun. Dialogue gives the effect
of real speech but with all the boring rubbish taken out.
Every thought you've ever had has been thought better and by
someone else. Does anyone have any questions? We talked
last week about the stanza, you might think of stanzas as little
rooms: what are you going to do in yours? Are you going to just
lie there watching light reinvent itself? The second line doesn't
scan. Yes, flair is better. For homework, sit in a soft chair and
describe the exact experience, no, don't do that, write down a
conversation you hear on a bus; go out in the rain and open
your mouth; make a list of everything in your bathroom cabinet.
Try not to break your line on an article. The first person
you have to please is yourself, but if nobody else is pleased
you have a problem. Fill out the form and give it back to me:
te-dum te-dum te-dum te-dum te-dum. Notice that beautiful line
where the widow's hands are likened to the wings of a dead bird.
Less is more, but sometimes less is less. What do librarians get paid?
I've never seen that particular noun used as a verb. But it's too late
now to get to grips with the Dewey Decimal System.
Did anyone else have a problem with the turnip metaphor?

Self-Portrait with Washing-up Glove

When the man with electrocuted eyes
leans towards me in the street and whispers
Stop trying to kill me,
I'm appalled but unsurprised:
it's what I've been telling my new neighbourhood all day –
its jumpy traffic lights
and muscled staffs, that pub where the end of the world

can't come soon enough. July: someone
in another postcode will be thwacking tennis balls. Here
the gobbed-on paving slabs wobble in the heat
and as evening falls Mister Chicken's
neon tux grows washing powder white. I turn right
into the never-ending street until the giant weed plant
waves to me like fallen royalty.

The hallway hamster smell remains, but some
of the worst is over: that splayed
biro shell has been picked from the sink, the chest
emptied of alien knickers, and gone is the bee on its back
rocking in a drawer by itself, legs crunched up
like a dog begging.
As I remove the freezer shelf, my neighbour
hollers at her child. A scattering of frozen peas
are stuck to something pink.

Oh God, we should amend our lives,
all of us who sleep in rented beds and deafen
at the mention of a pension plan;
all of us who've lived our best days
in the imagination's potting shed.

The oven is black inside
and I snap on a marigold, flexing my fist
like someone who might land a half-decent punch.

The Unborn

mooch about and waste time
starting things they'll never
finish. The next world
is nothing to them but shadows,
some don't have patience
for any of that crap at all –

What, *grass,* they say, waving
their wobbly arms, You mean
you actually believe in *grass?*

Heartsongs

The feathery hearts of the ill-at-ease
    Murmuring – startled – eager to please

The choux-light hearts of the oh-so-holy
    Filled with cream from a distant dairy

The twiggy hearts of the always-left
    Breaking stick by stick like nests

The wire grilled hearts of the ne'er-do-well
    How to get near them? Who can tell

The battered satin hearts of the sad
    Little empty evening bags

The heave-ho hearts of the undeterred –
    Rowing, rowing, never a word

Madonna of the Pomegranate

Botticelli c. 1487

Surrounding her, the sorrowing angels
turn in all directions
as if they know and dare not tell.

Once, I spent weeks
following the folds of her gown,
trying for a way to replicate
her curved mouth
and those averted irises,

but even though the sketch was fair
I came no nearer to the figures
bound inside the circle –

that adult-looking Christ child weighing down
his mother's arms,
the sweet fruit it so saddened her to hold.

In Service

Five days in this new position
and my duties so inexpertly
performed. You eye me
with no smile as I pat dry
your auburn hair. Your feet
I've rubbed with olive oil,
offered part-remembered songs,
knelt to nibble short your nails –
they unpeel soft as candle wax.

Attended to, you turn away
and I retire. Night drifts into day.
Your cry again. And so the work
of love is never done;
I gather up my skirts and run.

Hotel Pool

Twelve? Thirteen? She arrives
in advance of her parents,

fat as I was thin, wrapped in a towel,
pattering to safety –

a bench where she sits obscured
before abandoning herself

to the indecency
of a walk towards water.

(Though who's to see? To care?
The retirees? Me with my puckered stomach?)

My eyes meet hers,
hers dart away like fish;

this is not the place to say
You'll be all right,

the body must become itself,
nothing to do but swim out, follow.

When Six O'clock Comes and
Another Day has Passed

the baby who can not speak, speaks to me.
When the sun has risen and set over the same dishes
and the predicted weather is white cloud,
the baby steadies her head which is the head of a drunk's
and holds me with her blue eyes,
eyes which have so recently surfed through womb swell,
and all at once we stop half-heartedly row, rowing
our boat and see each other clear
in the television's orange glow. She regards me,
the baby who does not know a television from a table lamp,
the baby, who is so heavy with other people's hopes
she has no body to call her own,
the baby who is forever being shifted, rearranged,
whose hands must be unfurled and wiped with cotton wool,
whose scalp must be combed of cradle cap,
the baby who has exactly no memories
softens her face in the early evening light and says I understand.

In a Church

No, no time for this
the outside clamours to be heard,
the books, you see,
the books.
In here it's dark, the sun
has slid away.
There are necessities.
The cars are travelling at speed, without me, fast;
the days, my days, must be pinned down
accounted for and coloured in,
I need to go,
I need to go my way.

To which the soul said, *stay.*

Elegy for the Living

We wash up side by side
to find each other

in the speakable world,
and, lulled into sense,

inhabit our landscape;
the curve

of that chair draped
with your shirt;

my glass of water
seeded overnight with air.

After this bed
there'll be another,

so we'll roll
and keep rolling

until one of us
will roll alone and try to roll

the other back – a trick
no one's yet pulled off –

and it'll be
as if I dreamed you, dear,

as if I dreamed this bed,
our touching limbs,

this room, the tree outside alive
with new wet light.

Not now. Not yet.

Experience

The widow will weep for her beau, my dear
While the spring grass continues to grow, my dear

Life's lengthy or short but it ends when it ends
We arrive and we go and that's so, my dear.

The elected must govern, the masses must vote
Every man has his price (*quid pro quo*, my dear)

But God seldom bargains and never in Lent
For he's too busy fighting the foe, my dear.

The moon eats her heart out again and again
Though the rivers just go with the flow, my dear.

An earthworm divides well, a country does not
And sometimes a yes becomes no, my dear.

Our wishes all fall down the well with a splash
There are decades of echoes but oh, my dear.

Give up what is lost if you can't fish it back
Just keep walking. And that's all I know, my dear.

II

Life Coach Variations

The Life Coach Compiles a CV

Before he coached Life, he coached tennis
while also selling shoes.
He knows the inner game.
He understands the importance of a good fit.

The Life Coach Tends his Herb Garden

Lemon thyme thrives when watered sparingly.
Mint runs free.
But the basil is spindly and turning yellow,
which troubles him;
he has a hunch it will never prosper
but does what he can.

The Life Coach Bumps into his Ex-Wife

She's in a rush, he isn't.
He kisses her continentally
remembering to ask after her partner, Ray,
a thick-legged civil engineer.
In his raincoat pocket he squeezes
the peel from a tangerine.
All afternoon its pith bothers his fingers.

The Life Coach in Florida

Wintering. He snorkels;
sun burns his neck, frazzling
the curled white hairs on his shoulders.
An old friend waits on the beach.
For lunch there'll be fresh tuna,
scorched outside, inside practically raw.
He wonders if this is the life.

The Life Coach Visits a Relic

He queues to examine the saint's ankle bone
because he believes in curiosity.
But when he reaches the front
the bone is inside a box and the box is behind glass.

An elderly woman beside him is grasping a flower.
He leaves her to it. She kneels
and presses her palm flat to the glass,
touching whatever is or is not.

The Life Coach Travels on a Bus

He rarely uses public transport,
but when he does he tries to profit
from the experience. Even when stuck
at faulty traffic lights. *There is goodness
above me, there is goodness below me,
there is goodness beside me* he chants.
In front, the neck of a girl,
blonde down at the nape;
her lad places his finger there
and strokes. The life coach closes his eyes.

The Life Coach at the Pool

Whistles reverberate
as school kids thrash in the next lane.
His grandfather could cut through water
efficiently as Johnny Weissmuller;
both men left their native lands
to make their own luck.
His grandfather died unmedalled but still strong.

The Life Coach Passes a Woman on the Escalator

They know in that brief
meeting of eyes
there are children
they should have raised.

The Life Coach Considers Maslow's Hierarchy of Needs

Self-actualisation is the summit,
the illusive snowcap
to which every client aspires.
They look at him to haul them up –

he imagines himself on the mountaintop
as they might see him,
sunlight striking his wraparound shades.

The Life Coach Phones his Mother

These days he sometimes believes
she is already dead.
Their conversations are discordant,
full of echoes, pauses, repetition.
He closes his eyes and sees her young again,
planting pea sticks, her tumble
of brown curls.
Yes, I'm still here
she says into the silence.

The Life Coach Holds a Newborn

It surprises him afresh –
the frankness of the gaze:
as if she were looking through a
                            glass-bottomed boat
to assess the fish –
noting every blemish, every flash
of rainow skin.

The Life Coach Peels a Boiled Egg

After rinsing in cold water, he taps
and rolls, taps and rolls.
That light crunch before the membrane
glides free, like satin from
the firm white flesh of a woman.
Life is easier with technique.

The Life Coach Takes a Bubble Bath

A billion herbal bubbles break
against his thighs as he braves the sting
of the hot hot water. Lying back
he starts to solve a problem in the paisley
tiles. His muscles
loosen. Crystal clusters balance
on the springs of his chest hair
and vanish forever.

The Life Coach Writes a Sympathy Card

The blank space invites ink
yet he's cautious as a man testing his weight
against an icy expanse.
Words occur and drift away:
the wrong commitment
is usually worse than none.

The Life Coach Casts Himself as Trevor Howard

In the borrowed flat, Celia Johnson
slips free her scarf.
This time they're undisturbed.
        He unbuttons her dress,
presses his cheek imploringly
to the rising breast until – sordid
though it is – she cannot but give in.

The Life Coach on the Stairs

Halfway up, or down,
he forgets entirely what prompted this.
Objects of all descriptions float across
the nothing of his mind:
Sellotape? Screwdriver? Hat?
He might hover all afternoon,
become an African,
a woman, a tomato plant. What was it?
Are these even his feet?

The Life Coach Finds an Old Passport

He hardly remembers
where it took him, but recalls
Marta's mouth in a Baltic snow.
      Signature newly fixed,
occupation long abandoned,
the uncertain smile of a black-haired boy
who might have the look of his son.

The Life Coach Thinks in Haiku

The meaning of life
has something to do with sun
warming his forehead.

The Life Coach Chokes on a Boiled Sweet

...the suddenness of end
arriving now!
On his hands and knees he pants
with animal relief:
how absurd
to be ripped from this world
by a pear drop.

The Life Coach Paints a Self-Portrait

In the peachy light of the dining room
as the day forgets itself,
he makes a mark with charcoal
on paper from the art shop.
He runs a finger over his nose, cheekbones,
pulls the tuft of beard.
This is me, he says, squinting.
This is me.

III

Apocryphal

The end of time is approaching, but, like a country bus,
　　　　it'll come when it comes.
　　　　Other people die, apparently. We have actually seen it happen.
There are lists and box sets,
there are days when it might still be jacket weather or maybe
　　　　　　　　　　　　　　time for the coat.
Whatever they say on the forecast, can we really believe them?

The end of time, ah yes, it slips the mind,
there's only so much wisdom can be flung at it. Only so many quips.
Here it comes
　　　　in its ten-league boots
　　　　　　　　trampling all over our honorary degrees.

Beyond the headline but before the horoscopes, the story of a woman
who took a sip of chablis in a crowded top floor restaurant,
slipped off her shoes and stepped
　　　　　　　　into a late summer afternoon.

Remember the man who paced Oxford Street warning against
the dangers of protein?
　　　　　　He too has been swept to the end of the world,
　　　　　　　　　his sandwich board clacked cold shut.

It is coming. Make haste. Make hay.
Do nothing.

It is coming,
and all those puzzles which sit in our disorganised hearts will be
flung away
　　　　whoosh
　　　　　　each piece scattered to lie where it falls.

Who cannot be glad for the man in the baked goods aisle, glad
he had the courage
to put on his dress before it was too late?

Be glad, too, for the woman in the therapists' seated beneath a
                                        dripping spider plant:

there's time for healing yet.

Why aren't you building an ark?
                Why are you whitening your teeth?

The climate scientists will die regrettably in labs or on golf courses,
surrounded
by Portuguese sea, the tang of beer still on their lips.

The end of time is coming and we must walk out of our unhoovered
rooms where dust skeins shimmy our skirting boards,
we must walk away from the clod of unsorted washing, disregarding
                                                    that space

where we intended a pot plant to stand.

To her Unconscious

And besides all that, you're costing me money.
Am I speaking loudly enough? Is this supposed to be *funny?*
I know what Freud said about jokes
and I know what my mother said about Freud.

Am I speaking loudly enough? This isn't funny –
Kleinians don't come cheap.
My mother was right about Freud.
Stop it with that dream of Chairman Mao in the little red shorts,

what the hell is wrong with you? Kleinians don't come cheap.
I've got work to do, cakes don't bake themselves
and I don't have time for Chairman Mao, or his shorts.
You can also wipe that film of me in ballet class,

I've work to do, collapsible beds don't collapse themselves
and who else is going to sort the dark wash?
Yes, Mrs de Lancy's ballet class:
I can't keep wetting myself for the next forty years.

Mother said it all comes out in the wash
but quite honestly, she wasn't qualified to give advice
and I can't go on like this for another forty years:
I've heard about the stuff you get up to

while I'm busy trying to get advice
about the wobbly bathroom tap and I've had it up to
here. I know what Freud said about jokes
but I'm not laughing: you're costing me money.

The Daydreams

Mr Daydream says, It's not so bad after Wednesday is over with.

Once there was nothing: now there is a saloon car
and two deckchairs in the summer,
a dead cat buried under a rhododendron bush.

The days happen.
One day she's wearing an orange blouse and he loves her. The next
she's sighing, he thinks
I never wanted this — can't you make yourself more lovable?

Mrs Daydream has the words to old songs by heart, songs
that predate her mother, when girls in hats wouldn't stand
                                                    for saucy talk.

How they enjoy it when the trees dream themselves into leaf;
                        how they knit their fingers together and sigh.

Mr Daydream likes to take tea from a clean cup.
Mrs Daydream is lacking when it comes to washing-up.

Does somnambulist fit? She asks, glancing up from her wedding ring.

Mr Daydream can hardly remember life before the car,
                        the deckchairs and the dead cat.

Mrs Daydream thinks, It's not too bad once Sunday is done.

What I wouldn't give, says Mr Daydream.

There was the morning she pushed out and all the pieces of her life
fell to the floor like scenery. *Kerflunk. Kerflunk.*

Once Mr Daydream was beaten for stealing a fountain pen
                                        he didn't steal —
he remembers a mustard carpet all too well.

The word resentment makes Mrs Daydream think of a black acorn.

She recalls someone saying: It's heartbreaking
when perfectly decent people have no one to love.

The light in the bathroom pulses twice before it comes alive.

Hermits

They must be still among us;
Have they swapped
Their caves for caravans,
Wild honey for a scrape
Of margarine?
They must be sitting
Somewhere
Nursing silence
Like a warm egg,
Hopeful for its yellow meat,
While outside, what?
A distant A-road
Barely audible?
A washing line?
Where is it television
Doesn't come
And emails don't remind you
Who you are?
The place reserved for living out
The solitary offices of noon
And afternoon.
There must be someone now
Who sits as Julian
Before her sat
Passing a decade through
Her fingertips –
Does she see God
Reveal the world perched
In his palm, small as a hazelnut?
Does she turn
Towards the window
After dusk, alone and not,
To hear the birds call one another home?

Late December

Life brought me low.
Love bid me lift my head:
It rained and nothing
Flowered. Love laid
His hand on me. I burned.
Begin again he said,
And with the year, I turned.

Love Song in a Bleached Room

I wait a long time before Anya comes:
off-duty she smiles and my skin goes electric.
Take me home, I say through my unmoving mouth.

Aren't you asleep yet? She asks.
Not asleep, I say with my nearly dead lips.

There is a moon outside or no moon. The lawn
stripes with light or no light. In the pavement cracks
insects are living their unexamined lives.

Anya won't talk when she's tightening the tourniquet.
My veins are so fat I almost giggle –
swollen rivers to places I've forgotten existed.

She tells me not to think too hard,
it's bad for my readings. She charts me like a ship
despite the fact I'm anchored safely to the bed.
If you try to jump there's fuss –

the lifejackets taste of bitter rubber,
the lighthouse comes straight for your eyes.

Anya, If I say her name forty, fifty times, it means
nothing, it's merely sound let loose.
My eyelashes are on the brink of extinction but

my arms still work. Up down they go
when I ask them to. All right when I plead.

Anya knows my arms were not always like this.
I could sing once, I tell her with blinks,
show tunes and passages of light opera.

Her curls are shiny like ribbon
or frazzled with fatigue, and either way I wish
I could touch them.

The Grudge

Feed it first
with mustard spoons,
with care, avoiding
sudden and disarming light.

Sing, (you know its songs).
Gnnarr, it says. *Gnnarr.*
Little thing, little thing.

A daytime moon
and still you're there,
pink-eyed, the mustard spoons,

the tablespoons, while the grudgeless
dream bland dreams – and nights
of them – until

one evening? Afternoon?
(So many spoons),
you find it's grown,

it's strong enough
to bear you on its back
and ride you mightily
through this whole cold world.

The Hem

Matthew 9:20

Twelve years untouching and untouchable;
doctors clueless, conciliatory, bleeding her
until she's nothing left, drained, still bleeding,
she's willing to try anything,
        twelve years sticky rich with oxides,
and she finds the place.   But the crowds!
Every wretched man and woman, son and daughter,
blighted, clean,
shouting to a blot of someone. Him?
        Could he tell her what she'd done?
        Such an outpouring.
Though what had any of them done?
        She couldn't, could she, touch his arm, his hand?
Crawl then, she could crawl at least, and reach.
Twelve years gone, twelve years of waking stained,
unchanged, same blood orange sun, eclipsed now
        as she pushes forward in the dirt.

In the Woods

The baby sleeps.
Sunlight plays upon my lap, through doily leaves a black lab comes,
a scotty goes, the day wears on, the baby wakes.

The good birds sing,
invisible or seldom seen, in hidden kingdoms, grateful for the in-
between. The baby sleeps. Elsewhere the Queen rolls by

on gusts of cheer —
ladies wave and bless her reign. The baby frets. The baby feeds.
The end of lunch, a daytime moon. The leaves

are lightly tinkered with.
It's spring? No, autumn? Afternoon? We've sat so long, we've walked
so far. The woods in shade, the woods in sun, the singing birds,

the noble trees.
The child is grown. The child is gone. The black lab comes,
his circuit done. His mistress coils his scarlet lead.

Conversation with a Lime Tree

November afternoon. Sudden sun:
outside the lime
            only subject of our window frame
turns on like an electric lamp and asks
        Who lives here,
                    what do they do all day?

        I live here with my child, I say. We read about a plucky mouse
(a mouse who owns a house and does the hoovering, the mouse's
friends – a crocodile, an elephant – also own their properties).
I teach my child to say her name.

        The lime attends –
it has no home, only an environment, a street to which it lends
                        the accolade of leafy.
        Who are those others then, downstairs?

This house belongs to them,
        they've installed a burglar alarm
                and drive a silver car;
money flies from our account to theirs invisibly as dream, crinkly
as leaves, and while they sleep, it settles
                    keeping in the heat.
Settling, I tell the tree, Is key.

The lime gives its attention to a toy gorilla
                reclining on the sofa bed –
He has no name, I say, and go on to explain
    how things have changed since saplings
    flourished on this road,
    how the young and newly middle-aged may be adrift forever
like the Israelites, vanquished by the subprime,
                and no Moses anywhere to part
a sea of lack,
        nothing but Twitter plaguing their heads.
        Twitter? Says the tree.
Never mind.

Tell me more about the neighbours.
>They're nice. They sweep their leaves – our leaves?
>(Or mine, suggests the lime).
Their bins are orderly.

The lime digests this with a stripe of light, and asks
Is it difficult to love people?
>Sometimes, if you know their insides might be anything like
your own. If you're in a hurry, preoccupied, suffering a leaky boot.
Better to be a mostly speechless tree,
a tree whose insides are accounted for, a tree who does no harm
or has harm done to it.

>The lime won't be romanticised:
>ash dieback carries on the air. It has experience of
pollarding.

Our silence is companionable.

>Stratocumulus, a film clip comes to mind:
unmortgaged Mary Poppins rises
in a darkening sky, sails over London fog
>and chimney tops, a job well done, one to begin.
>Might she stop here?
>If I climbed the tree and waved her in?
Childrearing can be a lonely business in the modern age, I say.
Many weekend supplements have turned the subject inside-out,
>it costs for someone else to hold your child
while you pop out to work
>at being who you were.
The tree is listening with its twigs.

>Daytime telly's no replacement for a colleague
(studies show it's worse for everyone than intravenous drugs).
But you're
more sentient than the presenters of those shows, your lighting
more compelling.
>Changeling. Darling tree.
The lime shifts uncomfortably: it is an English tree.

What about community, have you ever fancied standing in a wood?
     Too mulchy. You?
I try to picture it, but can't. The amalgam of days
and how to live them, eh?

                 Is it time to join a commune, tree?
Is it time to commune far-off? Far from this unaffordable view,
unaffordable you?
     Somewhere a child could tumble without Wi-Fi wired to her,
where straw might muss her hair?
     Perhaps.
Is it time to learn to knit professionally? Is it time to buy
a narrow boat?
The lime withdraws to shadow.

          Have you no answers to our
wants and lacks and rented homes, our ragged bank accounts,
     the long grass where everything gets kicked?
     Tree!
Are you only here to make our furniture? To give us books, maintain
our warmth?
Are you only here to illustrate ideas of dignity,
            to keep our graveyards looking picturesque?

Don't be depressing, says the tree.
And please, don't shout.
     I offer my apologies.

A blackbird bounces on an upper branch,
                in time it starts to sing.

Lucid

In the struggle to escape that old brute, meaning,
she's way out in front:
truly we can't do what she does,
which is? Receive/return the world purely...
and by *purely?*

Critic, she *resists* meaning,
she *foregrounds* our part in meaning-making.
In short, we can make no sense of her, only follow
where she points.
There's no doubt, she's whimsical,
see? A random nose, or door, or rain, yes r-a-i-n!
At any moment will the thing-ness of it
pop into her mouth?

If we could return there just a little while,
to where she sits, fuddling her spoon,
but ahhhhh there's nowhere to go,

even in the shuffled picture book of dream, umbrella
won't be unhooked
from its stand,
our strings of syllables
can't be folded
like the stretchy wands magicians use.

Head bowed, she chews her own distinctive cud.
Head bowed, fixated by, what? Ah...empty crisp packet...

We gather in the doorway
patting ourselves down for words,
losing them like keys;
she chitters to her plastic cups, addressing
what passes in her vanishing language.

The Great Divide

Your kith and kin are listed in Debrett's,
my people eat their tea at half past five,
for I am from the land of serviettes

where no one hunts or cares for string quartets;
because of this I'll never quite arrive.
My kith and kin aren't listed in Debrett's,

they don't play bridge, they don't own salopettes,
your sort of fellows are not meant to wive
the sorts of girls who reach for serviettes.

Montgomeries are cut out for Nanettes,
and Quentins need Fenellas to survive,
(I know of this from reading your Debrett's).

Chin up old chap and let's have no regrets,
we've had some fun but let us not connive
to mix the napkins with the serviettes;

our fathers simply come from different sets,
these old divisions help a nation thrive.
Your kith and kin are listed in Debrett's,
and I am from the land of serviettes.

Kitsch

sees her name in lights, for she's a drama queen, naturally,
 – *Sing out Louise!* – but isn't straight vulgarity (lap dancing,
karaoke). She appreciates an audience, waves a teasing hand at those

who've trained, and understands the heritage of hoofing.
Kitsch is goofy, frequently. Kitsch stays late at parties, charms in
imitation fur, refills her Babycham repeatedly.

She dabbles in religion for the outfits, follows politics if there are
badges but says No to sport, unless bedazzled by the lure of gold.
Don't leave your kids with Kitsch, you'll return to find

they've razzmatazzed your wedding album and are jumping
tartrazined and feather-boaed on your hand-made Swedish bed.
Kitsch isn't shy of money but likes funny more. Kitsch over-

does it, free wheels, surface skims, rejoices in the faux;
she worships frippery, nostalgia, bawls her eyes out frequently
and falls in love in seconds flat. She can get tiresome, all that

me, me, me. Kitsch forgets your name, takes no notice where
you went to school, cries 'Life's too short' then shuffles off
to Buffalo in ribboned shoes. Kitsch is used to others gossiping

behind her back "*So* crass, *so* talentless." She has no use for subtlety,
no truck with lofty poetry, (Doesn't all that worthiness
just bore the pants off you?) Kitsch doesn't want to change the world

or fill your brain with big ideas, she only wants to make you *feel,*
she's all heart, after all, a heart forever pulsing, sentimental as
a Lourdes Madonna's, glowing ruby when you plug it in.

In Brief

She left her teenage lovers in their box rooms
smoking weed and sped towards the city,
splashed in light, her smile skew-whiff
beneath the banner heads, came to in hotel
suites and signed to men who taught her how
to hold herself while they held her. The
magazines stacked up – the premieres, the
tribute dolls, the fuss – before that stolen shot
of her in tracksuit pants, depressed,
barbiturates and supermarket hair, flights to
sealed clinics in the hills, palms spread like
jewelled starfish on the lens, the boys
returning, kicking back the covers of her past.

Forgiveness

I have done so many wrongs.

There is the woman who once loved me
and to whom I am dead, she appears
from a wooden clock
banging and banging her cymbal brass.

What do people do with absolution?

On a school retreat
a missionary monk said in his New York accent
If you knew what went on in my head,
but we knew he hung about piss-scented stairwells
looking for junkies to love,
and where did that leave us?

They are the old songs, the songs the therapists sing,
big band numbers gone tired.
Let it go.
But where can it go? I mean

if I turned out my heart like a pocket
you would find such things.

Once, I asked an actor for his autograph
and then discovered he was someone else.
Forgive yourself he said, taking my hand in his
as I searched out an exit path,
Promise me that you'll forgive yourself.

Nocturne

Midnight for the squirrels and the drunks,
midnight for you dear and your chest hair too,

put your pen down pet and rest here.
Midnight swallowing the mirror whole, swallowing

my mother in her pale blue slippers,
and my brother, my big brother in his too small bed.

Bed, the longed-for stopped-short sound delivering
us at last from sense-making. The trains

are empty, the magnolia trees are still, the tower block
has lost another dozen yellow squares but

they'll fill up and we'll fill too, and in tomorrow's
morning we'll awake, washed up again among

the bills. Meanwhile, the stars are queuing up
to get behind your lids. Come, give me your hand.

23

The Lord is my shepherd; I shall not want
for much. He maketh me to lie down
on the chalky grass of Finsbury Park, the skatepark
distant; he leadeth me beside the canal's still waters,
curtained barges settling, resettling,

underneath them sediment thick enough to spread on sandwiches.
He restoreth my soul until it is gold like the straps
of the sandals in Krishna's Shoes, shiny
like the sunglasses of the young.

He leadeth me in the paths of righteousness for his name's sake
(though I shuffle with the others
at the crossing, waiting for the good green man).

Yea, though I walk through the valley of the shadow of death,
or stand in the mirrored kebab shack alone at three a.m.,
or pass my father resurrected in the eyes of an aged vagrant
and wish myself his daughter, I will fear no evil:
for thou art with me; thy rod and thy staff they comfort me.

Thou preparest a table before me in the presence
of mine enemies – who may be numerous, though I seek
to drown them in love. Thou annointest my head with oil,

as I shampoo the baby's hair,
splashing my hand for her delight as outside
a deluge dashes the panes. My cup runneth over.

Surely goodness and mercy shall follow me all the days
of my life; on channel ferries
and through the aisles of antique markets; in the sallow
closed-off rooms of the sick; in playgrounds, family resorts,
and in precincts where the elderly collect.

And after the bungalow, the care-home, whatever awaits,
I will dwell in the house of the Lord forever.

Acknowledgements

Thanks are due to the editors of the following print and online publications in which some of these poems first appeared: *Best British Poetry 2012, Forward Book of Poetry 2013, Lungjazz: Young British Poets for Oxfam, The Manhattan Review, The Manchester Review, The New Welsh Review, The North, Oxford Poetry, Planet, Poetry London, Poetry Review, The Spectator, UEA New Writing*. I am grateful to The Society of Authors for an Arthur Welton Award, which supported the completion of this book. Thanks to kind friends, particularly Kathryn Maris, Sarah Ridgard and Jon Sayers. Thank you to Amy and the team at Seren. Special thanks to Todd Swift for his notes on the manuscript. But most of all, thank you to Stephen Keyworth.